ELEMENTS OF GEOGRAPHY

Environments

David Flint

HEINEMANN

Heinemann Library,
an imprint of Heinemann Publishers (Oxford) Ltd,
Halley Court, Jordan Hill, Oxford, OX2 8EJ

OXFORD LONDON EDINBURGH
MADRID PARIS ATHENS BOLOGNA
MELBOURNE SYDNEY AUCKLAND SINGAPORE
TOKYO IBADAN NAIROBI GABORONE HARARE
PORTSMOUTH NH (USA)

© Heinemann Library 1993

First published 1993
93 94 95 96 97 10 9 8 7 6 5 4 3 2 1

Contents

What is the environment?

The **environment** is the natural surrounding in which humans, animals and plants live. We are part of our own environment, so we must care for and protect it so it will sustain life far into the future.

There are many different environments around the world. The different environments are created by natural forces and by humans. When we talk about natural forces we mean temperature and the weather, for example. Some environments are deserts where there is low rainfall. At the North and South Poles, the environment is freezing cold and there is ice and snow all year round. The hot, wet rainforests near the Equator teem with life of all kinds. This environment is home to more than half of all the different sorts of plants and animals on the earth.

People affect their environments, too. We adapt our natural environment so that we can live there. In deserts, people make the land usable by adding water to the soil to grow crops. This is called **irrigation**. Where there are large rivers, like the *Nile* in Egypt, a lot of land can be irrigated. This provides a lot of food, and income for the farmers.

Very little can grow in the burning sand dunes of the hot deserts.

Humans can also harm the environment. Rainforests all over the world are cut down for their valuable wood. Also, people think that because so many varieties of plants grow there the soil is good for growing crops. When they cut down the trees, however, the soil is not fed by the **nutrients** provided by the forest and the crops fail. As rainforests are cut down, plants and animals are destroyed. Many species of animals and plants are now **extinct**.

Dramatic events can change the environment in just a matter of seconds. These can be natural disasters or caused by humans. Earthquakes, hurricanes and tidal waves cause widespread destruction. Sometimes, other disasters like huge oil spills from tankers rapidly change the environment. We must make sure that these disasters never happen. If we look after our environment, it will look after us.

The Antarctic is covered in ice. It is also dark here for six months of the year. Few animals can survive in this environment.

> **Did you know?**

Deserts cover about fourteen percent of the earth's land surface. Only about five per cent of the earth's population live in deserts.

Soil – the basis of the environment

The sun, frost and the rain all attack rocks. The weather breaks the rocks into smaller and smaller pieces. Soil is made from these pieces of broken down rock, **minerals** and **humus**.

> Did you know?

One handful of soil can contain as many as 1600 million bacteria!

For plants to grow well they need certain things from the soil. Plants need water, minerals and nutrients. Humus is very important because it helps to hold water in the soil. Plant roots take up this water. Bacteria live in the spaces in the soil. They are important because they help to break down the rotting material in the soil. This releases nutrients for the growing plants.

Wheat grows well on the fertile soils of the US prairies.

Ploughing breaks up the soil before the seeds are planted.

Soils are described by their colour and texture. The colour is due to the different minerals in the soil. Soils with a lot of iron in them look red. To judge texture rub a sample of soil between your thumb and finger. Sandy soils feel very gritty. Silt soils feel slightly rough and clay soils feel smooth when dry but are very sticky when wet. **Loam** is the name given to soils which are a mixture of sand, silt and clay. Loam soils often contain plenty of nutrients. They are deep and free from boulders.

○ Looking at your local soil

Collect a small sample of soil – enough to fill a jam jar. Tip it onto a newspaper in the garden. Spread out the soil and break up any lumps.

- Study the soil with a magnifying glass.
  Can you see any remains of plants or animals?
- What colour is the soil?
- Shake the soil through a wide-mesh sieve.
  This will leave pebbles and stones. This is the coarse soil. Weigh this.
- Now sieve the soil through a fine-mesh sieve.
  The soil left in the sieve is the medium soil. Weigh this.
- Weigh the soil that goes through both sieves.
  This is the fine soil.
- Make a bar graph of the amounts of coarse, medium and fine soil in your sample.

All soils have coarse, medium and fine material. The amount of each varies from soil to soil.

Soil in profile

Soil is made up of different layers, rather like a sponge cake. When you cut through a sponge cake you can see the layers of jam, cream and cake. In the same way when you cut through soil you can see different layers.

The top layer is usually dark brown. This is because it has a lot of humus in it. There are also lots of plant roots. This top layer is the most fertile part of the soil. That means it is the part which has most of the nutrients, minerals and water. It also contains a lot of soil animals like earthworms. Earthworms burrow their way through the soil. Air can get into the soil through the burrows, and water can drain away through them.

Lower down, the next layer of the soil is often pale brown. There are fewer plant roots here. There is also less humus. Lower down still there are bits of rock in the soil.

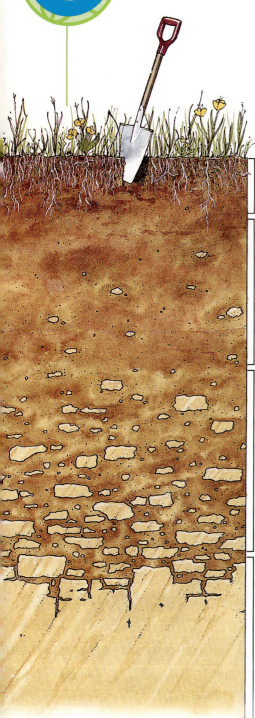

Root layer

Soil

Broken-down rock

Solid rock

A soil profile.

> ➢ **Did you know?**
>
> If a worm is cut in half, then the half with the saddle (the fatter pink piece) will survive.

The steep slopes of high mountains have poor soils.
Little grows on these mountainsides in the Himalayas.

○ A soil profile

You will need an adult to help you with the digging.

- Pick an area of ground away from trees and dig a hole in the soil. Look at the top of the soil. Measure how far down the plant roots are.
- Dig down as far as you can. Make the hole big enough to see the sides. Make the sides vertical with the spade. Look at the different layers of the soil. Notice how their colour varies.
- Use a ruler to measure the depth of each layer.
- Take a piece of wood 1 metre long. Divide it up into the same depths as your layers of soil.
- Coat the surface of the wood with a layer of glue (not superglue).
- Scatter a small amount of soil from each of the layers in your profile onto the correct place on the piece of wood. Now you have a record of what the soil looks like in each layer.

This is your **soil profile**.

Soil erosion

Soil erosion is the removal of the top layers of soil by wind or water. **Wind erosion** takes place when strong winds blow over fields where the soil is not protected by vegetation (trees, plants, crops). The loose top soil can be blown away in huge dust storms. This happened in parts of the US prairies in the 1930s. An area known as the Dust Bowl was created where the soils were badly eroded.

Water erosion takes place when heavy rain falls on a soil surface not protected by growing plants. Sometimes the water can wash away the soil across a whole field. This is called **sheet erosion**. The soil ends up in streams which carry it away.

Dust storms can blow away tonnes of soil in a few hours.

This dust storm in the US prairies in 1936 buried houses under soil.

Soil erosion is sometimes called 'the silent crisis' because people may not be aware that it is happening, until it is too late.

Experts believe that soil erosion may be made worse by the way farmers use the land. For example, leaving the soil surface bare means it is exposed to erosion by both wind and water. Growing the same crop on the same field year after year can lead to soils becoming exhausted. They have less humus and so are more easily eroded. Cutting down hedgerows exposes the soil to the full force of the wind.

Soil is a valuable resource on which we all depend. Farmers have to look carefully at how they use the soil to prevent any further erosion.

> ➤ **Did you know?**
> Fields in Shropshire can lose as much as 3–4 tonnes of soil per hectare every year!

Stopping the rot

Soil takes thousands of years to form, but it can be blown or washed away in just a few years. Soil erosion causes the top layer of soil to be washed or blown away. The top layer is the most fertile part of the soil (the part with most nutrients). If this top layer is removed, only the lower, less fertile, layers are left behind. These layers have much less nutrients. Crops do not grow well on soils which have been eroded. Eventually it may be impossible to grow crops in some fields because there is no top layer of soil.

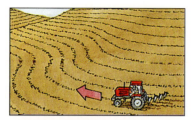

Plough along a slope, not up and down.

Plant hedges around fields.

Plant crops in rows.

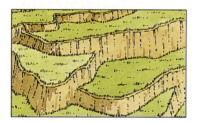

Build terraces.

Don't leave land bare.

Use natural fertilizers.

Farmers' advice on how to stop soil erosion.

Streams and rivers flowing through the eroded area become full of soil. The soil in the water causes the whole river to change. Less sunlight filters through the murky water. Plants in the water need sunlight to make food for growth. These plants also produce oxygen as part of the process of growth. Without sunlight, the water plants cannot grow and so cannot produce oxygen. This means there is less oxygen in the water. As a result fish and animals die.

To stop soil erosion farmers have changed the way they use the land. Now they plough along slopes and not up and down. This slows down the water drainage away from the field, and so slows down soil erosion. In other places, shelter belts of hedges and trees have been planted around fields. These hedges break the force of the wind and so cut down the amount of soil that can be blown away.

Steeper slopes are terraced to prevent erosion. **Terracing** involves building a wall across a slope and filling in behind it with soil. Again this slows down water drainage from the fields.

Farmers now leave the top soil covered by a crop for as long as possible. This protects the top soil from wind and water. Other measures to prevent erosion include planting fast-growing bushes in gulleys.

Terraced hillsides in Portugal help to stop soil erosion.

A river system

The place where a stream or river begins is the **source**. Usually streams and rivers have their sources in hills or mountains. Some rivers like the *Nile* in Egypt have a lake as their source.

Water in a river or stream flows downhill. Most rivers eventually flow into the sea. As the river flows onward other streams join it. These streams are called **tributaries**. They make the main river deeper and wider. The area of land that supplies water to a river is the **drainage basin**. Some rivers, like the *Mississippi* and the *Amazon* have drainage basins which cover thousands of square kilometres.

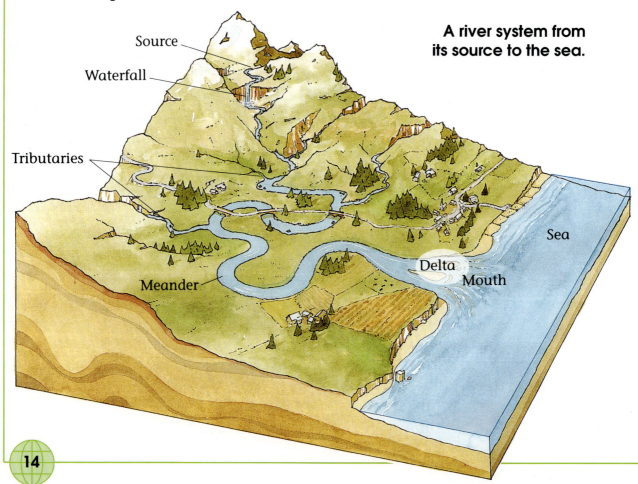

A river system from its source to the sea.

Near its source the river is usually fairly shallow but flows very fast. Pieces of rock are carried along with the swirl of the water. These wear away the rock to form a channel. After heavy rain the river can carry along huge boulders. The pieces of rock carried along by the water grind against each other. They become smaller and more rounded. Eventually they may be broken down into fine sand or even mud.

As the river flows toward the sea, it becomes wider and deeper. As it does so the river bends from side to side. These bends are called **meanders**. On the outside of the bend, the river flows very quickly. Material from the bank is worn away. On the inside of the meander, the river flows more slowly. Here sand and mud drop out of the water and build up on the river bed.

Rivers form meanders on their way to the sea.

At last, the river reaches the sea. The point at which a river enters the sea is called its **mouth**. As it flows into the sea, the river slows down. It drops a lot of the sand and mud that it has been carrying. Sometimes this sand and mud builds up to form new land, called a **delta**. Eventually, the delta grows so big that the river has to split into channels to flow around it.

Waterfalls

Niagara Falls.

Waterfalls are formed when a river plunges over the edge of a steep drop in a shower of water. Waterfalls are one of the most dramatic and spectacular natural sights in the world. The falling water makes a huge roaring sound as it crashes down to the river below. A fine spray of water rises like mist or smoke from the waterfall and drifts over the surrounding area.

➤ Did you know?

Niagara Falls is actually two waterfalls; the American Falls and the Horse Shoe Falls in Canada (shown above). The Horse Shoe Falls are the wider of the two and plunge down 54 metres in a torrent of spray and foam.

Waterfalls are found in places where a layer of hard rock lies on top of a layer of soft rock. Gradually the soft rock is worn away, leaving an edge of hard rock over which the water tumbles. Most waterfalls are found near a river's source. Here, the river is fast-flowing and carves its way through hilly areas. The water tumbles over the edge of the drop straight down into a pool at the bottom. The water and pieces of rock swirling around at the foot of the waterfall wear away a hollow. This hollow is called a **plunge pool**.

A **cascade** is the name given to a waterfall with a small amount of water or a series of waterfalls, one after the other. **Rapids** form when there is a mixture of hard and soft rocks on the river bed. The water wears away the soft rock and the hard rock is left jutting out, causing the water to swirl around.

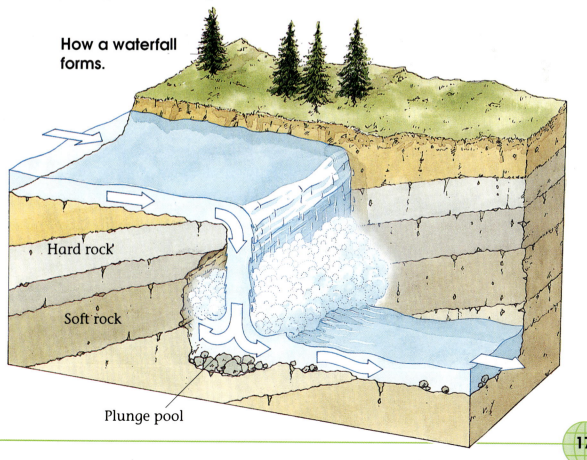

How a waterfall forms.

Hard rock

Soft rock

Plunge pool

Floods

Heavy floods in North Wales in 1990.

After heavy rain, a river carries much more water. The river level rises and at some point may spill over its banks. The water floods the surrounding area of flat land. This area of land is called the **flood plain**.

The flood plain is usually very fertile. When the water has drained away, it leaves behind the sand, silt and clay it has been carrying. This fertilizes the soil. But living on the flood plain can be dangerous. In some places like Bangladesh, many farmers live on the fertile land of the flood plain. In times of flood when the river overflows, crops are destroyed. Homes are often damaged or washed away.

People have built defences to stop the flood water. The Aswan Dam in Egypt controls the flow of water to the flood plain of the *Nile* below. People are now able to irrigate their land and farm it in safety. The dam also has another use. The water flow through the dam generates enough **hydro-electric power** to supply the whole of Egypt. Although this dam helps to protect people living on the flood plain, it does mean that this land does not receive flood water regularly. Now, instead of the flood plain being fertilized naturally, the farmers have to use artificial **fertilizers**.

Some rivers are in danger of flooding at high tide. In 1982, a flood barrier was built across the *Thames* in London. This protects the area at risk from flooding.

> ## ➤ Did you know?
>
> The *Huang He* (*Yellow River*) in China each year carries enough sand and mud to build a wall one metre high by one metre wide 27 times around the earth!

The huge Glen Canyon Dam in Arizona holds back flood water. It also generates hydro-electric power.

Polluting our rivers

The water in rivers all over the world is being polluted. Some of this **pollution** is caused by factories which dump waste chemicals into rivers. For example, in the river *Rhine* in Germany, dangerous chemicals like cadmium have built up. This has caused the fish to become sick and die.

Chemicals are often sprayed on crops to kill insects or other pests. Not all these chemicals are used by the plants. When it rains, these chemicals may be washed away into rivers. On some farms huge amounts of liquid animal manure, called **slurry** may seep out of its containers and into a river. Slurry has killed all the fish, plant and insect life in long stretches of rivers.

Fertilizers washed from the land have caused the rapid growth of red weed in this river. This causes there to be less oxygen in the water and fish and other animals die.

A field of flowers is sprayed with chemicals from the air.

People are very concerned that many of the world's rivers are polluted. Laws have been made by the European Community which will cut down water pollution. Water is vital to all life on earth. Without it people, animals and plants could not survive. The water we drink has to be treated before it is safe. This takes place at a water treatment centre. Here, the water passes through a series of sand filters called **filter beds**. These filters remove some of the impurities in the water. Next, chemicals like chlorine are added to kill off any harmful bacteria. The water which people use for drinking, cooking and washing becomes pure and free from pollution.

Polluting our land

Coal is an important resource. It is burned in power stations to make electricity. A lot of coal around the world is now mined from open-cast sites. In **open-cast mining**, huge digging machines scoop out the coal that lies close to the surface. These machines can lift as much as 50 tonnes in one scoop. They then load the coal onto big trucks which carry it to the power stations.

Open-cast mining is a cheap way of getting coal out of the ground. Coal that lies deep underground is mined by sinking deep shafts. This is a very expensive type of mining. Many underground mines have now closed.

> **Did you know?**
>
> Britain has enough reserves of open-cast coal to last for over 150 years.

DANGER BLASTING

Open-cast mining can cause many problems in the countryside.

Many people feel that open-cast coal mines pollute the land. Large areas of countryside are dramatically changed by the mine. Fields, farms, hedgerows and woods all disappear, to be replaced by a huge hole in the ground. As more and more coal is mined, the hole gets deeper and wider. When the mines are abandoned, these holes fill with water. This makes them very dangerous, especially for children playing nearby.

People have different views about open-cast mining.

Open-cast mining creates a lot of dirt, dust and noise. The coal is often blasted so that it is loose for the diggers. The air can become full of dust. The big lorries which carry away the coal can cause other problems. On narrow country roads the lorries add to the danger of accidents and traffic jams.

Restoring the land

What happens when the coal from an open-cast mine runs out? British Coal owns most of the open-cast sites in Britain. They are keen that old mines do not become dangerous eyesores. In some cases, British Coal want to return sites to their earlier use as farmland. In these cases the open-cast mine is filled in and fertile top soil is spread over the area. Farmers are able to use the land either for growing crops or for rearing animals. In this way, Britain actually gains some farmland each year.

A working open-cast mine.

Some open-cast mines have been landscaped and remodelled. Trees have been planted on hills newly created out of rock and soil. Special areas have been developed for wildlife. Ponds have been made, where in the past there were just holes in the ground. The land around these ponds has been planted with seeds and bushes. The ponds have been stocked with frogs, toads, dragonflies and fish.

Watersports are being developed on newly-created lakes.

Some larger pools have been used for watersports. New roads, launching areas and even leisure centres have been built around these new lakes. There is now a big demand in Britain for places where people can waterski, sail, fish, windsurf or race powerboats. At the moment there are not enough lakes and reservoirs around the country to develop these watersports. The new sites created from old coal mines are very welcome.

> **Did you know?**
Each year British Coal restores over 2000 hectares of land for leisure and use by farmers.

The Albert Dock

The Albert Dock in 1981, before its revival.

Ports are very busy places with lots of industry. They employ many people. Just like other parts of the environment, ports can become run-down. But they can also be revived. This has happened to the Albert Dock in Liverpool.

By 1981 Liverpool had become less important as a port. Some modern ships had become too big for Liverpool's docks. The water was just not deep enough. Fewer ships came to Liverpool. The factories and warehouses which depended on the goods carried by the ships were forced to close. By 1981 Liverpool had a large area of empty docks and derelict factories. The whole area was run-down and vandalized. The dock gates were broken and the docks had filled with mud brought in by the tide. This mud was polluted by sewage and chemical waste.

By 1992 all this had changed. The Albert Dock had been transformed at a cost of £110 million. Now the Albert Dock has modern shops, offices, wine bars and restaurants. In 1988, the Tate Gallery North

opened in the site area. The exhibits of modern art attract over one million visitors each year. In 1991, the new Merseyside Maritime Museum in the Albert Dock buildings was visited by 2.4 million tourists.

The revived Albert Dock and Maritime Museum.

The docks have been repaired and cleaned up. Canoeing, windsurfing, dinghy sailing and even yachting are now found in Liverpool's docks. Plans for the future include a national aquarium, a roller skating centre and a water theme park.

Improve your environment

A blue tit carries an insect back to its nest.

Our local environment needs a lot of attention. This will make sure that the world around us is as beautiful as possible. It will also ensure that wildlife like birds, insects and animals can live there.

You can improve your environment. The first step is to carry out a careful survey to see what is there already. A map is useful here. You can mark on it important areas like ponds or streams or trees. For example, try to identify which trees are in your area. How many different species are there? Where are they? What size are they? Do they look healthy?

➢ **Did you know?**

In one week in December 1992, people in Britain planted one million trees to improve the environment!

Think carefully about how you might improve your environment. You could create a wildlife area in part of a garden or park or even part of the school grounds. Let the grass grow long here and form seeds. This will attract birds like greenfinches which live on the seeds. Allow nettles to grow. In summer they will attract insects like butterflies. In turn, this will attract insect eating birds like blue tits.

You may want to plant some bushes in your wildlife area. **Buddleia** bushes are very popular with bees and butterflies. **Cotoneaster** and **pyracantha** bushes have brightly coloured berries in autumn. These will attract birds like thrushes and blackbirds. You may also be able to make a small pond. Lots of birds will come to drink and have a bath. Your pond may even be visited by fabulous insects like the dragonfly. A pond will also be very popular with frogs and newts. Don't forget to leave some shallow water around the edge of the pond. This will make sure that the animals can easily get in and out of the water. Try to make sure that at least one part of the pond is over one metre deep. When the pond freezes in winter, the frogs will be able to survive in the mud of the deepest part.

The dragonfly begins its life as an egg in a pond.

Glossary

buddleia Bush with fragrant flowers attractive to butterflies.

cascade A series of small waterfalls.

cotoneaster A bush which has bright red berries.

delta Area at the mouth of a river, formed by deposits of sand, mud and silt.

drainage basin Area of land that supplies a river with water.

environment The surroundings of people, plants and animals.

extinction The wiping out of a species.

fertilizers Natural or artificial substances added to the soil to improve plant growth.

filter beds Filter beds at water treatment centres remove impurities from the water.

flood plain Area near a river which is flooded when the river level rises.

humus Decaying plant material in the soil.

hydro-electric power Power produced when generators are turned by running water.

irrigation System of supplying water to the land from rivers or reservoirs through ditches or pipes.

loam A fertile soil containing clay, silt and sand.

meanders A winding curve in the course of a river.

minerals Naturally occurring deposits of substances like iron, uranium, silver or lead.

mouth The part of a river where it flows into the sea.

nutrients Substances that plants need for growth.

open-cast coal mining Removal of coal deposits from the surface, rather than from mine shafts.

plunge pool	Hollow formed by erosion at the foot of a waterfall.
pollution	The release of substances that spoil the environment.
pyracantha	A thorny bush with bright-coloured berries.
rapids	A fast-flowing section of a river or stream, where the water flows around jutting rocks.
sheet erosion	Erosion of the soil in a whole field or area.
slurry	A fluid form of manure.
soil erosion	The removal of soil by wind and/or water.
soil profile	A section of soil cut vertically from the surface to the solid rock.
source	The place where a river or stream starts.
terracing	Forming a series of flat areas on a slope which can then be used for growing crops.
tributaries	Streams or rivers flowing into a larger river.
water erosion	The erosion of soil by rain.
waterfall	A sudden fall of water over a step or ledge.
wind erosion	The erosion of soil by the wind.

Index